Mike B Warm-ups!

The indispensable handbook for singers and choral directors

Contents

© 2002 by Michael Brewer
First published in 2002 by Faber Music Ltd
Bloomsbury House
74–77 Great Russell Street
London WC1B 3DA
Music processed by Richard Emsley
Illustrations by Harry Venning
Design by Nick Flower
Printed in England by Caligraving Ltd
All rights reserved

ISBN10: 0-571-52071-5
EAN13: 978-0-571-52071-8

To buy Faber Music publications or to find out about the full range of titles available
please contact your local music retailer or Faber Music sales enquiries:

Faber Music Limited, Burnt Mill, Elizabeth Way, Harlow, CM20 2HX England
Tel: +44 (0)1279 82 89 82   Fax: +44 (0)1279 82 89 83
sales@fabermusic.com   fabermusicstore.com

Introduction

WHAT ARE WARM-UPS?   Warm-ups are a series of activities that get the body and brain into gear and introduce healthy and effective singing practice at the same time. Whether you are a solo singer, chorister or conductor, warm-ups will enable you to use your voice more effectively and therefore transform your sound.

If you regularly use warm-ups already, this book will help you explore new ways to use them successfully. (More general trouble-shooting tips have been covered in *Kick-start your choir*.) By warming up properly, you will find rehearsals and concerts easier to manage and a lot more fun.

BASIC PRINCIPLES   We all learn in different ways and each singer will respond to different stimuli. Some people need to understand the physical processes before enjoying an action, while others respond instinctively and are less interested in the techniques involved. The best option for most of us is a combination of the two. Ten to twenty minutes is an appropriate length of time for warming up the voice effectively, but beware: if you don't know much about the muscular activity involved, ask an expert in order to avoid damaging activities. Similarly, if you make sounds that in any way hurt the voice: stop.

Some basic principles apply to all warm-ups and their use in rehearsal:

Stamina is as important in singing as in sport. Good muscular balance will make singing for long periods easier and keep the voice healthy.
Total involvement of the body takes pressure off the vocal apparatus, increases control and flexibility, and improves awareness.
Reinforcement of every activity in warm-ups and in rehearsal encourages the singer to perform instinctively.
Extremes are worth visiting. Do an exercise that takes you further than you need in the music; this will then improve control in the normal range.
Tune up not only the ears, but also muscles. Relax the jaw, neck and shoulders and calm the mind—create a balanced and comfortable posture.
Change things often, because variety improves flexibility and the ability to respond.
Harmony is at the centre of music making, so link each aspect—posture, breathing, sound-making, expression and communication—into one art.

HOW TO USE THIS BOOK   The warm-up sessions are arranged progressively; by working through them in order you can build on all aspects of technique a bit at a time. Alternatively, make a note of technical demands within the music that you are currently rehearsing, then select activities relevant to these demands from several sessions accordingly. To make this easier, icons indicate the specific technical aspect that is being targeted in each warm-up. These are:

 Posture: how to stand and sit efficiently and healthily.

 Breathing: using support from the whole body to manage the breath.

 Sound-making: starting, maintaining and finishing a sound.

3

 Range, register and resonance

 Velocity, virtuosity and flexibility (of the lips, tongue and jaw)

 Harmony and blend

 Body, mind and spirit

All the activities will help develop your tone and intonation, and you will find that a positive and physical approach will solve many problems within any piece of music.

Throughout this book you will come across music examples with chord symbols above them. You may find these useful when warming-up with an accompanist. Furthermore, numbers above the stave indicate that the warm-up can be sung in canon, when used in a choral context. Note: to make the warm-ups easily accessible, we have chosen to use U.K. English vowels rather than phonetic spellings, and hope that the examples will be clear to worldwide readers.

AND FINALLY ... The following warm-ups are examples and not prescriptions, so be creative and adapt each one to suit the particular needs of your choir. Remember that the best warm-ups are those you have created to help with music you are working on now! Incorporate specific phrases to be learnt, and match musical needs to skills. Think realistically about what your singers could achieve in the time available, prioritize, and change the emphasis in each rehearsal. Keep them guessing what's coming next!

ACKNOWLEDGMENTS My hearty thanks go to literally hundreds of choir directors and singing teachers from whom I have learnt constantly over the years. My inspiration began with Cyril Somers and Noelle Barker, and I have learned much from Pamela Cook and Vivien Pike. My thanks go to Rita Paczian for Germanic methodology, and to Robert Isaacs for American wizardry. Most of all I owe a huge debt to the National Youth Choir members and teachers: to Jane Highfield for her enlightened approach, and to the Betty's team of Deborah Catterall, Felicity Cooke, Tim Rhys Evans and Jebbie Williams for incredible cooperative brainstorming. Thanks to Sandra for her meticulous proof reading and to Simon Halsey, Kathryn Oswald and Richard King for their vision in getting the idea in place. Thanks also to Rosie for being a regular guinea pig, and to thousands of workshop participants for constant quality control! I hope you will have fun with this book, and that it may offer some help along the way.

— SESSION 1 —

SITTING PRACTICE

Try sitting firmly with your feet flat on the ground and stretch tall. Notice the strain on the lower back? Now sit back against the chair. It feels comfortable for a few moments, but do you feel the muscles around the waist collapse? Instead, sit with your centre of gravity above the toes (tuck your feet in, rest on your toes and keep your back straight). You can also sit forward with your bottom away from the back of the chair and feet flat on the floor. Make sure you can feel your thighs involved in supporting your weight.

STANDING UP

An inefficient way to stand up is by pushing yourself upwards, leaning on a hand. Can you feel the strain in your back? Instead, go back to sitting with your weight on your toes, and push yourself gently upwards by straightening the legs (thigh power!). Keep your back straight, but not tense. Practise this standing movement several times.

WHOLESOME BREATHING

Breathe naturally and lightly. Put one hand on your lower abdomen with the thumb on your navel and feel where the air goes (it may help to lie on your back). Enjoy the sensation of air apparently 'filling' your back. Gradually increase the strength of your breathing, feeling the increased expansion in your lower back. Blow your breath out with lips slightly forward, producing a constant sound.

STARTING A SOUND

Be a monkey: flex your knees, relax the shoulders, swing your arms and relax the jaw (with lips open and slightly rounded). Enjoy this posture. Make gentle 'cooing' sounds on any vowel at varying pitches, keeping them short. Create a little monkey poem of *oo* and *ah* sounds, keeping the rhythm free. Repeat this to the vowel *o* (as in *dog*, with the lips slightly rounded).

THE BEST MEDICINE

Start and release each note cleanly with even breath support. Repeat each bar/measure several times. Start at a slow tempo, then try a little faster. Repeat the exercise with different vowels, then at different pitches (for example: G, A, B♭, C and back down again).

OVER THE RAINBOW

Make the word *wow* into an exciting sound and throw it overarm in a rainbow shape. Then make a sound like a siren up and down from the top of your range (using the head voice) to *yeeaa*!

TONGUE TWISTING

Say quickly:

The tip of the tongue if it slips will eclipse both the lips as it flips.

Now sing it to this tune:

— SESSION 2 —

BALANCED STATURE Stand with your feet slightly apart (at five-to-one on the clock face) and feel how you are 'grounded'. Be a pair of scales and sway from side to side, returning to the most comfortable, central position, with your weight balanced equally on both feet. Don't sway when singing though! Make sure you stay balanced.

BREATH TEST Breathe deeply, standing or sitting, and place your hands on your ribs at the side. Then try with them on your lower back. Feel how much movement there is all round. You can also lie on your back to check if it feels the same (it should!). Think from the lower back and abdomen up, to give a feeling of 'wholeness' in supporting the sound.

 ACTION Breathe in, pulling on imaginary chest expanders, and release the tension slowly as you let the air out.

 TWO SPEED GEARBOX

Keeping the tempo slow, sing *oo* with lots of *hhh* first, then reduce the *hhh*, and finally, sing without it. Can you feel the difference? Repeat the exercise in different keys using the vowels *aw*, *o* (as in *dog*), *ah*, *eh* (*egg*), *i* (*if*) and *ee* (*feet*).

 A THOUGHTFUL HUM Hum *mmm* as a siren up and down—it is probably sounding mainly in the throat. Repeat, breathing in through the nose, then out with an *hhh* down the nose, starting quite high and falling (*hmmm*).

 ACTION Feel the vibration of your nose-bone as you release.

 ROLLER COASTER Siren gently to a *hm*, then *wow*, *yow*, *zoom*, and sounds of your choice along this line:

 ACTION With your arms held in front of you, push down on the rail of a roller coaster as you go up and let them float up as you coast down. Start with a slide at no particular pitch, then try it over the interval of a major second, major third, perfect fourth and so on.

— SESSION 3 —

GOOD SITTING CHECK — To check that you are really sitting straight, imagine a vertical line down from your ear, through your shoulder and hip, to the middle of one foot. Hold the position for a few seconds, then relax.

BREATHING IN PAIRS — Place both hands on your lower back with your thumbs on your waist. Breathe in and out, and check for movement. Some people may say they feel no movement. If so …

Repeat the game with another singer, one standing behind the other. Place a hand each side of the other's ribs, with thumbs on the lower back and hands around the lower ribs. Folks will reassure each other that something is happening! See if you can sense an all-round expansion when breathing in, and contraction when breathing out.

THE MORE IT GOES THROUGH THE NOSE … — Hum an *nn* with your hand over your lips, blocking the sound from your mouth. Repeat, this time covering your nostrils, and notice what happens. Keep your jaw relaxed and teeth apart. Now try this pattern:

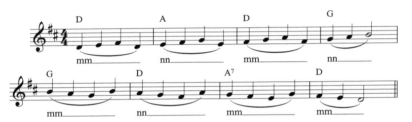

BASEMENT BARGAIN — Sing the following to *yah*:

Imagine you are holding imaginary chest expanders whilst doing this exercise, pulling them out as you go down the arpeggio. This will co-ordinate the support muscles (see **Tips and terms**, page 40) all round the body, and help produce an even and active tone.

FLOWER POWER — Sing the following to *wah*, then *zah*:

Throw each sound as a flower to a bridesmaid. Repeat as a staccato game, throwing smaller bits of foliage.

A SILENT SCREAM — Scream silently, then squeeze your face as small as possible. Repeat, changing suddenly from one to the other. Then flap your lips and tongue to make a *blwa* sound (as in the French *blois*).

Flap your hands, then arms, then the whole body!

— SESSION 4 —

SITTING TALL (THE WEEBLE GAME) Sit upright with your back away from the back of the chair and bend your upper torso from the waist, feeling the support from your thighs. Then rotate the trunk lightly, moving from side to side or making circles.

HIGH NOON Stand, feeling that you have a very long body. Lift your ribs, tilt your pelvis slightly forward, put your shoulders slightly back and feel the strength in your lower back. Feel wide!

BREATH MANAGER Breathe in gently, and blow out through the lips, maintaining an even sound. Check the support as before (see **Breathing in pairs**, page 6). When we talk normally we use quite a small amount of breath. For singing we need to use more, and to be more aware of how we manage it.

NATURAL GEAR CHANGE Say *I hear thunder*. Now sing these words to the tune of *Frère Jacques*. Repeat, gently touching the front of the neck. Do you feel how the position is different when singing? The larynx (see **Tips and terms**, page 40) naturally tilts forward when we sing, and remains flat when we talk.

EVENING OUT Sing the following to *ah*, *eh*, *oh*, *oo* and *ee*, keeping the vowel and your head position the same each time:

 Push down on an imaginary vaulting horse whilst going up, and hold a globe of light whilst descending. Repeat this warm-up to hummed *mm*, *nn* and *ng* sounds.

ARM'S LENGTH Sing *ah* fairly high in the voice and glide down as low as you can reach.

 Hold the sound in your palm and bring your arm down as you siren down. Then do the opposite; lifting your arm slowly as you siren down.

SNAKE TONGUE Waggle your tongue stretched forward between the lips. Say nonsense words like *biddle blather blub blub blub*. Now say the following, putting your tongue out between each syllable:

The theory of relativity is nonsensical to traditional mathematicians.

— SESSION 5 —

 MILITARY BEARING Stand straight. Be aware of straight lines of support—ears in line with shoulders, head relaxed, and eyes looking straight ahead. As before (see **Good sitting check**, page 6), imagine a straight line from your ear, through shoulder and hip, to the middle of your foot.

 SLOW MOTION Breathe in slowly through the mouth to a silent count of five, and out to a count of ten, feeling the evenness of airflow. Punch very slowly downwards with one hand against imaginary resistance as you breathe out. Now repeat, this time breathing through the nose. The golden rule is to create freedom in the sound-making part of the body.

 ANYONE FOR TENNIS?

Slur each five-note phrase, using a vowel (see **Tips and terms**, page 40) of your choice, keeping the tone completely even. Repeat to *nee, neh, nah, noh, noo, zee, zeh, zah, zoh, zoo.*

 Make a forehand tennis shot at the beginning of each phrase. Stroke the ball on the consonant and make a smooth circle with the racquet ready for the next stroke. Notice how light the semibreves/whole notes can be—this is the ball in the air, not landing on the ground!

 BABY TALK Sing on one note to words that emphasize the mouth/nose resonance alternation. Examples are: *mamma, nanna, manna, manamana, animal, enema, enemy, anemone, onion, banana, panama* etc. Enjoy the tongue movement, as babies do, and sing each word as you go up a scale.

 COLOUR SLIDE Sing the following once through, then try making up your own words.

yew yew yew yew yew yew yew yew   (etc.)

 A VOCAL SANDWICH Say *bread and butter* four times, as fast as you can. Then sing the words to a scale: first the whole phrase on one note, then two syllables on each note, then one syllable on each note. In a choral context, sing in canon after two repetitions of the phrase. Make up other phrases, and try with the conductor or a chosen chorister calling one and the rest answering.

— SESSION 6 —

MAXIMUM HEADROOM   Stretch tall, lifting the arms slowly above the head and stretching them to their full extent. Now stand on tiptoes and stretch even taller.

FLUTTER   Say *fft*, first gently, then more dramatically. Feel the lower abdomen with one hand, and then place the forefinger of your other hand half way between the navel and the breastbone, on the upper part of the stomach. Test what happens there. Repeat, this time with a hand on the lower back, thumbs on the waist and fingers forward. Feel the muscles at the side as the ribs expand, supporting the breath. Repeat to *flutter*.

    Imagine you have a bag of feathers hanging below each hand. Flick them up with each *fl* sound.

LIFT GOING DOWN

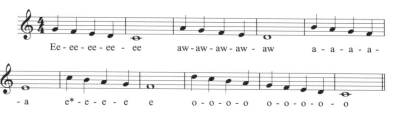

Ee - ee - ee - ee - ee   aw-aw-aw-aw - aw   a - a - a - a-

- a   e* - e - e - e   e   o - o - o - o   o - o - o - o - o

* 'e' as in 'egg'

Siren (see **Over the rainbow**, page 4) down on each vowel. Repeat with the same sound to the scale pattern above, and then try the exercise staccato.

    Starting with them at waist height, let your hands (palms upward) lift the counterweight slowly as you go down in the lift with each scale.

LEVERAGE

Ni - mi - nee no - mi - nee   ni - mi - nee no - mi - nee   ni - mi - nee no - mi - nee

ni - mi - nee naw

Put your energy into the consonant (see **Tips and terms**, page 40), letting the vowel bounce off it. Then try the warm-up again, using *jiminee, piminee*, etc.

   Pull a lever towards you with alternate hands on each dotted crotchet/quarter note beat.

PIECE OF CAKE

Black-ber - ry ga - teau and cho - co - late chip,   black-ber - ry ga - teau and

cho - co - late chip.

Sing with flexible lips and tongue. With your choir, create more cakes, and have groups perform a cake call-and-response! You could even give a prize (a piece of cake?) for the most inventive.

— SESSION 7 —

HORSE RIDING POSTURE
Imagine you are sitting on a horse. Hold the reins firmly and balance, letting yourself gently bounce as you ride. Try it with the horse walking, trotting, cantering and finally, galloping! Feel the all round control and balance that can be achieved whilst still sitting down.

FINGER TEST
Blow out onto a finger held in front of your mouth. Feel the smoothness and evenness of air hitting the finger and listen to the sound of air blowing through the lips. Test the breath support by putting your hand on your back, sides and stomach in turn.

A RINGING HUM
On one note, sing *ring*, holding the *ng* sound. Now take the sound *ng*, and glide up and down gently in the middle of your voice over the interval of a fifth. Repeat a semitone higher each time. This activates the soft palate (see **Tips and terms**, page 40).

ACTION
Feel the tingle in your nose. This enhances resonance and thus the clarity of words when we sing.

SWAN SONG
Call *whee!* slowly, and feel the tingle at the back of your neck.

COLOUR CONTROL

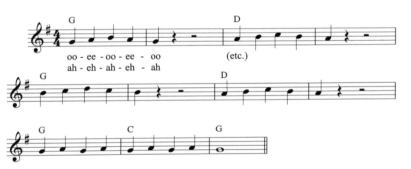

oo - ee - oo - ee - oo   (etc.)
ah - eh - ah - eh - ah

Keep the tone even by being aware of a constant breath flow (see **Finger test**, above). Then make up your own pairs of vowels.

RESONATE AND RELEASE
Resonate nasal consonants into vowels, and enjoy the release of sound. Secure the pitch of the consonant and feel it enter the vowel:

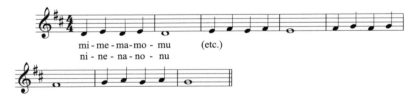

mi - me - ma - mo - mu   (etc.)
ni - ne - na - no - nu

PHILOSOPHICAL NONSENSE
Sing this nonsense song on one note:

Aristotle lost his bottle when he spied an axolotl.

Repeat with four syllables on each note of a scale, getting progressively faster!

ACTION
Flap the lips and tongue tip to make the words even clearer.

— SESSION 8 —

FINGER POWER Rub your fingers together until you can feel the circulation. Then flex them and rotate your wrists, elbows and shoulders, making increasingly big circles. Feel the freedom in each joint.

ON YOUR TOES Stand up, stretch upwards, and balance on your toes like a ballerina. Hold the position for a few seconds, then relax.

SHORT PANTS Using one long breath, breathe out in short pants to a whispered *hah*. Make sure that the airflow is gentle and even. Repeat to *ss* and *ff*.

 Hold an imaginary feather and flick it upward in alternate hands.

CABER CAPERS Siren to *wow!*, *yeeaow!* and *nyeeow!* Remember to aim for a feeling of resonance and openness in the throat.

 Try holding the sound with both hands, like a large log. Flick it firmly forward from behind the head with your palms upwards. Hold the log in front at waist height again in two upward palms, taking the imaginary weight in the whole body, and pull the log quickly towards you as you siren.

HAY CHEWED Sing slow descending triads to *yah yah yah*, then *yaw yoo yeh yee*, ascending by a semitone each time:

ya - ya - ya   (etc.)

Feel your tongue, lips and jaw working and enjoy even resonance through sustained breathing.

 Lazily chew a haystalk while you sing.

GETTING THE RING Practise singing *ring*, *singing*, *young* and *among* to a scale, then an arpeggio. Pause on the *ng* sound each time. Now sing this tune:

A - mong   the   young   the   sing - ing   is   bring - ing   the

zing   of   the   spring   in   the   songs   they   are   sing - ing.

RAG DOLL Let your arms and body gently fall forwards, gradually bending from the neck to the waist. Slowly unbend again, imagining the movement of each vertebra, until you are in a standing position again. Slowly lower your arms to the side, the front or the back.

SOUND LIBRARIAN Breathe slowly, then more quickly, then in short pants. Whisper *hhh*, *fff* and *shhh* (imagine you are a librarian!). Move one hand to different positions around the back and ribs, and check the muscular activity there. Enjoy the engagement of your body in the breathing process.

FRICTION AT WORK Revise *ss ss ss*, then *ff ff ff*, *th th th*, and *fft fft fft* (fricatives). Try them all at different speeds and volumes.

KEEP YOUR VOWELS REGULAR Say *oo*, then *ee*, then alternate—first with exaggerated lip movement, then more focused. Now try the following tune, combining lip and tongue action with smooth breathing and clean vowel sounds. Make up your own pairs of vowels too, and repeat at different pitches.

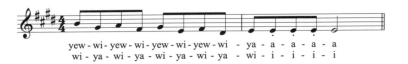

yew - wi - yew - wi - yew - wi - yew - wi - ya - a - a - a - a
wi - ya - wi - ya - wi - ya - wi - ya - wi - i - i - i - i

THE POWER OF *ng* Slide each pair of notes on the *ng* syllable. In a choral context, perform the piece as a canon, with each voice entering two bars/measures apart.

Hun - gry hun - ters sing__ a song__ and
bring__ a - long__ a bang - ing gong.

STOP THE CONSONANT! Make up rhythmic patterns that include the letters *p*, *t* and *k* (unvoiced plosives), and repeat them. For example:

If you've a packet of kippers then keep it apart in your pocket.

Or:

Particular stickers attract active vicars.

— SESSION 10 —

SPINDLE ARMS Extend your arms to the sides with your fingers held out straight, and begin to rotate them forwards. Gradually increase the size of the circle, before decreasing again. Feel the control in the upper arms. Repeat, rotating the arms backwards.

LET IT HAPPEN Breathe in and then slowly expel as much air as you can (it will be less than half the content of the lungs, honest!). When you have deflated as far as you can, let the pressure go. The lungs will fill of their own accord. Expel the air again, hold your breath and release. Rejoice as your whole breathing apparatus expands to let the air back in. Just let it happen!

SILENCE IN COURT Make long sounds on *sh*, and revise breath support (see **Tips and terms**, page 40). Whisper words, connecting the vowel to the *sh*; as in *shoo*, *show*, *shore* and *shy*. Make them long and even. In a choir, whisper this to your neighbour on each side then pass it along, filling the room with sound.

INTERVAL DRINKS Slide smoothly up and down intervals of a fifth. Check that the sound is supported and the tone even. Repeat the warm-up to *nn* and *ng*.

mm (etc.)

AFRICAN RHYTHMS Soloists, try these warm-ups one at a time. Choristers, get into groups and try all three at once. Vary the pitch, for example: group 1, high; 2, middle of the range; 3, low. Then change round.

tu - ta - ti - ka - ta - te, tu - ta - ti - ka - ta - te

pu - ku - tu   to - to - to, pu - ku - tu   to - to - to

pa - pa   pa   pa   pa   po - ke

14

— SESSION *11* —

EVER DECREASING CIRCLES

Rotate your arms from the wrists, then the elbows, then the shoulders. Try clockwise, then anticlockwise, each with increasing and decreasing circles.

LET GO

Breathe in gently, and as you breathe out count to twenty out loud, at about one number per second, all in one breath. Hold the breath for a second or two if you can, and then let go to allow the air to flow back in—it should happen automatically! (see **Let it happen**, page 13).

WIND MACHINE

Make a continuous *shh* sound, as your mouth changes from a smile to a whistling position. Listen to the change of pitch. Repeat, using *ch*, *whee* (a glide, like a swanee whistle, rising in pitch) and *shw* (falling in pitch, unvocalized). In a choral context, let each chorister change the sound independently to create a wind machine poem.

THE JOY OF DIPHTHONGS

(See **Tips and terms**, page 40). Say these words, lengthening the main vowel, and shortening the other: *blame, shake, lake, field, peeled, mice, rice, round, sound, ground, hear, near, home grown, use*. Now try *union, anoint, tune, neume* and *ointment*. Say them first, then sing to a scale. A good technique is to hold the first vowel through the whole note, and treat the other as a short equivalent of a consonant. For example: *my* becomes *maa-y*; *house* becomes *haa-wss*.

DIPHTHONG SONG

Try singing this song in a folk-style, with long second vowels, for example: *mayyyd*. Next try with long, Italianate first vowels, for example: *maaayd*. Try switching from one to the other.

My maid is late a - gain: my mind's in pain.
I will not take the blame: it's quite in - sane!

LEGATO WAITRESS

Enjoy an imaginary long drink. Sing a slow scale, up and down five notes, then six, then eight. Sing *ah*, changing to *mah*, then *zah, wah, la,* etc. Repeat a semitone higher each time.

Rest each long note (or a legato phrase) on a tray and pull it very slowly towards you. Make the sound beautiful as you carry it.

LINKING THE HEMISPHERES

Try singing a scale while silently counting the number of windowpanes, patterns on the curtains or anything else in the room.

— SESSION 12 —

LEG SHOW — Balance on one leg. Rotate the other leg clockwise, then anticlockwise. Start from the ankles, then from the knees, and finally the hips. Increase and decrease the size of the circles. Then try the other leg.

EVEN LONGER OUT-BREATH — Repeat **Let go** (page 14), this time counting to thirty at the same speed.

TONGUE TEST — Siren gently up and down in the middle range of your voice, using different vowels. Choose from *ww, oo, oh, aw, ah, aa, eh* and *ee*. Sing each one as a triad, ascending by a semitone each time. Enjoy the subtle movements of tongue, lips and jaw.

PITCH OF THE HISS — Say *ss* whilst opening and closing the mouth slowly, but keeping the teeth together. You will notice that an open mouth gives greater resonance. Try some important words containing *s* in your music, and decide on the mouth shape (for example: *sanctus* with a 'closed' mouth, or *dies irae* with an 'open' mouth).

LURVE SONG

While stars still shine I'll make you mine, our lives en-twine.

Repeat this exercise at different pitches, in different accents. For example: posh English, Texan, German, Liverpudlian, *etc.* For evenness and legato, sing the long vowels with an unchanged mouth position for as long as the note will allow.

PITCH NUMBER GAME — Sing a scale, ascending and descending, to the numbers one to eight. Now replace one of the numbers with a *sh*. Repeat several times, either changing the *sh* number, singing *sh* on two different numbers, or in canon, two beats apart.

BLOW YOUR CARES AWAY — Slowly drop your chin to your chest, conscious of the stretch at the back of the neck. Lift your head slowly as you breathe in equally slowly. When upright, gently blow, and your worries will vanish.

FREEING THE SHOULDERS   Rotate the shoulders backwards, forwards, together, separately, extremely and slightly. Do this carefully and with variation so as not to overuse particular muscles. Try varying the shapes.

INTERNAL COUNTING   Blow out gently, counting to twenty in your head. Let your lungs fill again naturally.

FINDING *ee*   Glide to *yeeah*. Repeat, holding the *yee* on for longer.

ACTION   Put two fingertips on the back of your neck, in the hollow below your skull, either side of your spine. Can you feel the resonance on the *yee*?

BOUNCE AND CATCH   With gentle onset (see **Tips and terms**, page 40), float the sound and lift the end of each crochet/quarter note. Sing to each vowel in turn. Try this in canon at one bar/measure, and then at four bars/measures:

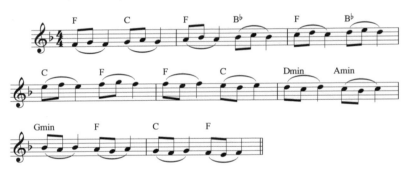

ACTION   Bounce an imaginary ball on each pair of quavers/eighth notes and catch it on the crochet/quarter note.

NONSENSE   Try this exercise in a canon of up to four parts, each a bar/measure apart:

ni - nga   na - nga   ni - nga   na - nga   ni-me ni   ni-me ni   nu - nu
nu - nga   no - nga   nu - nga   no - nga   nu-me ni   nu-me ni   nu - nu

BALANCED SCALES   Split the choir into two groups. Each group then sings a chosen vowel, or hums from opposite ends of a scale, simultaneously. Repeat in four groups, with each pair in thirds.

PRESIDENTIAL EXAM?   The old trick: with the palm of one hand, draw imaginary circles flat on the top of your head and with the other, tap your stomach in a regular pattern. Then reverse the hands.

— SESSION 14 —

THUMB SIGHTING Extend your arms to the sides, one thumb up and one down. Turn your head slowly to look at the upward thumb, then swap thumb positions and turn to look at the other one. Feel the muscular freedom and the comfortable limit of movement.

THE LAST COUGH DROP Repeat **Linking the hemispheres** (page 14) counting to thirty and then adding a very gentle cough at the end, to lose the final portion of air. It is important not to take in too much air; let nature decide the right amount.

THE SEARCH FOR *oo* ① Sing *oo* on a G in mid-range. Notice that the tongue is up at the back and right down at the front, with a big space above it, reinforced by forward and rounded lips.
② Now glide the *oo* up and down again.
③ Glide up and down the interval of a third, fourth then fifth. Change key by semitones.

Place your hands horizontally, palms down, with your fingers pointing to each side of your chin. As you sing, push the air slowly upwards with the backs of your hands. Listen to the sound as it changes and keep the jaw relaxed. Can you hear the increasing resonance in the room?

ANOTHER EVENING OUT This warm-up helps the vowels to sound even:

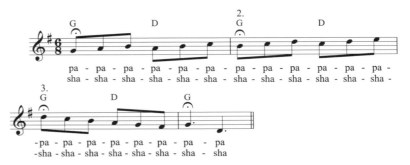

pa - pa - pa - pa - pa - pa - pa - pa - pa - pa - pa - pa -
sha - sha - sha - sha - sha - sha - sha - sha - sha - sha - sha - sha -

-pa - pa - pa - pa - pa - pa - pa - pa
-sha - sha - sha - sha - sha - sha - sha - sha

BUBBLE BATH This helps with range, co-ordination of sound-making, and lift. Be sure to articulate the separate notes and gently feel your abdomen at work. Repeat a semitone higher each time:

bro*_____ eh___ (etc.)

* 'o' as in 'broth'

Lift the energy of the sound, by flicking bubbles from the bath with your palms upward.

RHYTHM IN THE BODY March on the spot.

- Say *one two* in time with your left and right feet.
- Sing your favourite warm-up, marching at the same time.
- Try saying *one two three* so that the *one* falls on the alternate foot each time.

Remember that rhythm is in the body, so don't just count it—feel it!

NODDING DOG

Repeat **Thumb sighting** (page 17) very slowly, breathing deeply as you move your head. Repeat, making little waves with your head as you move it from side to side.

QUIET PLEASE

Breathe in through the mouth and feel the cold air touch the soft palate (see **Tips and terms**, page 40) at the back of the throat. Hold the breath for up to five seconds, before letting it release to *hhh*. As the air passes through the larynx (see **Tips and terms**, page 40) it may make a breathy sound. Make it even more breathy. Now release the jaw and tongue into a neutral position, and breathe in gently through the mouth. Can you do it silently? Ensure that you always keep the jaw relaxed.

AW, SHUCKS!

Sing *aw* (*or*) on one note. Feel how the tongue goes up in the middle. Now sing a gliding *aw!* as if surprised at some new gossip. Practise *ee-aw* in a sad voice and think of thistles. Now sing in gliding fifths up and down.

PLOSIVE WALTZ

This exercise involves the lips, front and back of the tongue. Start slowly and repeat it faster, a semitone higher each time.

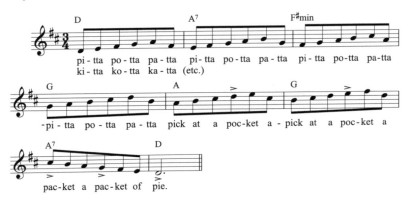

pi-tta po-tta pa-tta   pi-tta po-tta pa-tta   pi-tta po-tta pa-tta
ki-tta ko-tta ka-tta (etc.)

-pi-tta po-tta pa-tta   pick at a poc-ket a - pick at a poc-ket a

pac-ket a pac-ket of pie.

Try it in canon after two bars/measures, and make up your own nonsense phrases such as:

Picking a topical tropical topic.

CONFUSE THE BRAIN

Put your left hand on your right ear. Then put your right hand on your left ear over the top. Then bring your left hand from underneath and, over the top, put it on your nose, then on your right ear. Now do the same with your right hand. Carry on in this manner, and see if you can catch anyone out!

— SESSION 16 —

 LOOK LEFT, LOOK RIGHT With your arms at your sides, move your head very slowly from its forward position to looking over your left, then right shoulder.

 DRINKING GAME Imagine you are holding a large mug with a handle, containing your favourite beverage. Take a big drink from it. Hold yourself in that position and check the sensation. You should feel a sense of openness in the throat—this also works when singing.

 eh **AND** *air* Sing from *eh* to *air* (French *é* and *è*) alternately, on the notes F, G, A, G, F in the middle of your voice. You will feel the tongue lifting and falling, and find that the closed vowel *eh* (see **Tips and terms**, page 40) is much easier to resonate. Then sing a scale to *yeh yeh yeh*.

 With your index fingers, find the hinge of the jaw on each side and feel the buzz of the *eh* as you sing *yeh* to a glide.

 THE LETTER *L* Say *bell*. Now say the *ll* sound on its own, long. Sing it on one note, then glide it up and down. Make sure the sound is supported and feel the resonance in the neck and ears. Repeat a favourite warm-up or the melody of one of your repertoire pieces, entirely to *ll*!

 RUSSIAN SNOOKER SONG Sing this as a round and stroke the long consonants:

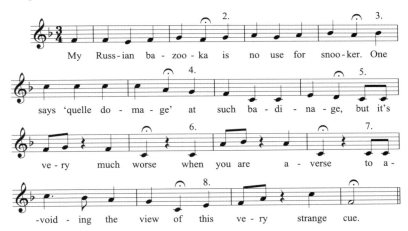

 CLAPOMETER March on the spot whilst counting out loud. Then replace the number one by a clap. For example: *[clap] two three four*. Now try *[clap] two three four five*. Now try counting silently, making sure that everyone claps together!

— SESSION 17 —

HEAD AND SHOULDERS Repeat **Look left, look right** (page 19) turning your head and shoulders together. Hold the position for five seconds at each extreme, then slowly release.

NOSE BREATHING Breathe in gently through the nose. Feel the air travel through the nasal passages and into the throat. Then say *hmm* with a glide, as if really enjoying your dessert. Enjoy the vibrations of your septum (nose bone).

VOICED CONSONANTS Say *zh* (voiced *sh*) as it would be said in Russian (like a French *je*). Feel how the making of the sound expands and vibrates the chest. Say it both long and short. Then try:

- *zz* (voiced *ss*), checking the front of the neck with one hand.
- *vv* (voiced *ff*), checking the sides of the neck with two hands.

CONFETTI Make sure that the onset (see **Tips and terms**, page 40) to the first note is gentle. Lighten the second note, and release with a quiet, staccato crochet/ quarter note. Keep the resonance high as you descend. Repeat a semitone higher each time, to vowels of your choice, slurring as marked:

a— a a— a (etc.)

  Scatter confetti, making circles with both hands. Start at the waist and move up the body, floating down freely on the crotchet.

FAST TYPE One vowel per note, sing *a* (as in *apple*), *o* (*dog*), *i* (*fish*), with open mouth (tongue down) and *oo*. Then *ma*, *mo*, *mu*. Then *za*, *zo*, *zoo* and so on, using other consonants.

  Type firmly on an old-fashioned typewriter on every note.

— SESSION 18 —

 TRUNK LINE Look slowly round behind you to the left then right, moving your trunk. Repeat this exercise, breathing in as you look round and out as you return.

 FLOWER SENSATION Breathe in through the nose, and imagine that you are smelling a flower. Feel the fresh open sensation from nose to throat. What is the temperature of the air?

 THE ELUSIVE _o_ VOWEL Say _dog, frog, log_, then just the _o_ on its own. Make a monkey poem out of it, then sing it to a scale up and down. A good philosophy is: 'All Os are _o_ (as in _dog_) unless otherwise decided'.

 OPEN DOOR POLICY Sing the following to _daw (door)_, then any consonant and vowel of your choice:

 ACTION On the second quaver/eighth note of each pair, open a door in the back of the neck and let the sound float upwards.

 VOICE YOUR OPINION Say _bah!, dah!, gah!_ strongly. Enjoy the implosion of lips, front of tongue and back of tongue respectively (but not respectfully). Repeat **African rhythms** (page 13) replacing the _t_ with _d_ in the first phrase, the _p_ with _b_ in the second, and _p_ with _g_ in the third phrase.

 NOT BACH AT ALL Sing this in canon at one bar/measure in up to four parts:

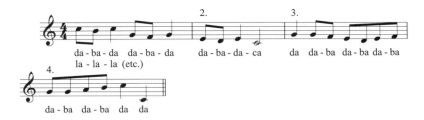

Now trying singing these sounds instead of the words in some music you are learning at the moment.

 YOUR CALL March on the spot, counting out loud to five continuously. The leader signals (by raising a hand) a different action to replace a number. For example: when the leader's hand is raised, call out _hoi!_ So the pattern might be: _[clap] two hoi! four five_ in one sequence, and _[clap] two three hoi! five_ in the next.

SWIMMING Crawl (or freestyle!) with fully stretched arms, making big strokes and taking each one across the front of the body. Lift the corresponding heel off the ground as the arm comes over, and time them with the length of each breath.

QUICK INHALATION Breathe in quickly through the mouth then call *hi* to a friend across the room, using a 'singing' voice—don't shout. Repeat to another friend (if you have two!) in the next room. Check whether the sound is supported, *i.e.*, whether you can feel movement in the back, abdomen and chest. What is the temperature of the air you breathe in?

SHIP'S HOOTER Make a sound through pursed lips, like a ship's hooter, until the top lip tingles. Now open the lips slightly and adjust the sound to make a clear *ww*.

A STROLLING HUM Sing to *mm*, then *nn*, then *ng*. Choristers can sing this in a four-part canon, one bar/measure apart, ascending by a semitone on each repetition:

  If space allows, stroll around whilst singing, gently swinging your arms in half-bars/measures.

HIGH COLOUR Sing up and down a triad on the vowel *i* (as in *hit*). Repeat a semitone higher each time, until you reach the top of your comfort zone. At this point you may find that modifying the vowel (see **Tips and terms**, page 40) slightly (to *eh* or *uh*) makes the note easier to sing, and to listen to! Repeat to other vowels of your choice.

FEED THE BIRDS This warm-up helps to place vowels through the range. Repeat a semitone higher each time. (Darken the vowel on top F sharp and above to avoid harshness.)

shee shee-ah shee - ah, shee-ah, shee-ah, ah ah__ ah__ ah

  Throw bread with alternate hands, and watch it arc over the pond.

TRIPLE-TASKING March in minims/half notes, and count out loud to six in crochets/quarter notes. Clap once on every offbeat.

TRIFFID — Draw imaginary pictures such as faces, stars or screensavers of your choice on the ceiling with a pencil attached to the top of your head. Then gradually bend forward, unwrapping your vertebrae. Sway like a triffid or a weeping willow in the wind, then slowly return to a standing position.

RESONATING REINDEER — Sing *i i i* (as in *bit*) on one note and place your hands at the side of each cheek with the fingers upwards.

Slowly raise your hands upwards and backwards past your ears, growing antlers as you sing. Feel the sound resonate.

THE SCURL OF THE *rr* WITH THE PING OF THE *i* — Roll your tongue to say *rr*.

① Press a doorbell firmly and let it *rrring*.
② Make siren and revving noises.

Be aware of the resonance in the neck and power at the hinge of the jaw by feeling them with your hand. Then try this exercise, with each vowel in turn, moving up a semitone each time:

SUSPENDED ANIMATION — On one breath, sing this warm-up through once to each vowel. Repeat in different keys.

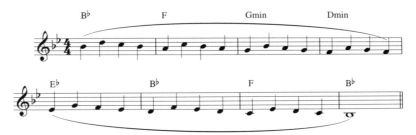

ESCALATOR — March in crochets/quarter notes, singing up and down a scale to numbers. In a choir, divide into two groups with each starting from opposite ends of the scale.

THE INDIAN ROPE TRICK   Imagine you have a rope attached to the top of your head that goes over a pulley in the ceiling and back down to your hands in front of you. Gently pull on the rope and feel your neck and shoulders loosen as your head's weight on your neck is eased. Try this sitting down, then slowly stand up as you gently pull on the rope.

MORE SWIMMING STROKES   Practise breaststroke, using strong upper arms to propel your body through resistant water, and breathing in time to the stroke. Now try backstroke with the same feeling of power.

JUGGLER   Say *j* (as in *judge*) and *qu* (as in *quackers*), and check for abdominal movement. Make up a rhythmic game, mixing these with other consonants (use **African rhythms**, page 13, if you prefer).

 Juggle oranges with each sound. Throw each sound to your neighbour, catch it on an in-breath and then throw it back.

DARK CHOCOLATE   On one comfortable middle note, slowly darken from *eh* (*hair*) to *uh* (*her*). Feel *eh* in the jaw hinge, and enjoy the space as the jaw opens and the middle of the tongue drops slightly towards *uh*. Repeat a semitone higher each time, until you reach the top of your range. Notice at what pitch it starts to feel easier to sing the darker sound. In the music you are studying, this is the place to start modifying the tone.

MONKEY-CALL RAG   Gently whisper *kah* sounds, varying the vowel with liquid lips. Enjoy the variety of sound colours you can make with minimum effort. Choristers can sing the **Monkey-call rag** in a canon at two bars/measures, and finish when everyone reaches the last bar/measure:

DUKE OF YORK   March in crochets/quarter notes, whilst singing numbers up and down a scale in minims/half notes. In a choral context, divide into two groups, and have group two starting on the third minim/half note. Then divide once more into four groups; two groups ascend like this in thirds, whilst two groups descend simultaneously. Repeat, singing sol-fa, pitch names, or sounds of your choice.

— SESSION 22 —

MORE SWIMMING Do the butterfly stroke and free up both arms together. Change the stroke on someone's signal. Then revise **Triffid** (page 23) and when bent over, breathe slowly several times and feel your back expand.

SIGNAL EARLY Make the following sounds: *ah* (dentist visit), *air* (short for *air hair lair*; a posh person greeting a long-lost friend), *ee* (a Yorkshireman expressing surprise), *aw* (American sees small furry animal) and *ooh* (pleasant surprise). Practise the start of any vowel exercise from a previous session. Make the mouth shape of the first vowel you will be singing before you breathe in—just like a violinist holding the bow in readiness to play!

ITALIAN LOVE Basic italian vowels require 'open vowel' singing (see **Tips and terms**, page 40). Be sure to place the consonant *before* the beat and the vowel *on* the beat:

A – mo – re.

GLIDING ACROSS THE RANGES Sing the following phrase, gently lifting the sound over the register changes. For fun, yodel the same tune, then repeat the gliding version, a semitone higher each time. Take each vowel, then add consonants such as *ya, fa, sha, va, yeh, feh, your, four*, etc.

BELL TOLLS March or clap crochets/quarter notes. Sing a scale up and down to numbers, or note names, or tonic sol-fa. Divide into two groups with each singing alternate notes. Hold them on to make bell sounds.

STUTTERING DUCK Say, then sing, the following. Choristers can sing this as a canon at two bars/measures, then at one. Try it with all parts on unison G, then with several parts at different octaves. Then build a triad. Try it a tone apart, or even a semitone! Make up other sounds and whisper them, then speak them with unpitched accents before repeating the process above.

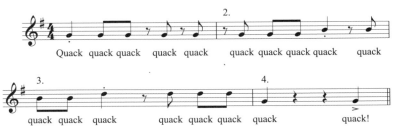

Quack quack quack   quack quack   quack quack quack quack   quack

quack quack quack   quack quack quack   quack   quack!

— SESSION 23 —

PIECE OF FLUFF Breathe in gently, then blow an imaginary piece of fluff from a wrist or a candle flame. Do the same again with a hand on the lower back, then the lower abdomen, then the top of the stomach below the ribs, and finally, on the chest and shoulders. With luck, everything but the shoulders should move!

VOWEL VARIATION WITH TALENTED TONGUE Sing to a slow scale, ascending:

*   Sing *oo* and lift the tongue (sounds like a gentle *r*).
*   Sing *ah* and lift the tongue (becomes *air*).
*   Sing *air* and lift the tongue (becomes *eh*).
*   Sing *ee* and drop the tongue (becomes *eh*).

TABLE TENNIS Sing *ba*, *da*, *ga* and every other vowel in turn, to different rhythms. Sing at increasing velocity. Check your breath support and then repeat very softly and very loudly. Then sing the following (choristers can try it in canon at two bars/measures):

da - ga - da   da - ga - da   di - gi - dee   di - gi - dee   (etc.)

  Play table tennis with a neighbour, batting each sound at the half-bar/measure.

ROUND THE MULBERRY BUSH Go round the sequence of vowels as follows, one step in each case: *i-ee*, *ee-eh*, *eh-uh*, *uh-ah*, *ah-o*, *o-aw*, *aw-oo*.

Sing them:

*   In middle voice on one note.
*   Sliding upwards.
*   Sliding downwards.
*   In a rainbow from low to high and back.

Merge the vowels by gradual change. Sing in parts, starting at different times.

ON AND OFF Sing a scale up and down. On a signal, change to silent singing and back again when the signal is given again. Speed up the frequency of the signals, and see who you can catch out!

— SESSION 24 —

SHAKE IT UP Shake every joint you can find, standing on flat feet then on the toes.

PAPER CHASE Blow firmly. Imagine you are blowing a piece of paper across a table, or inflating a balloon.

VOWEL VARIATION WITH GENTLE JAW By using the jaw alone, we can dramatically alter the sound of a vowel. For example:

- Sing *ee* and open the jaw, to form *eh*.
- Sing *oo* and open the jaw, to form *aw*.
- Sing *ah* and close the jaw, to form *uh*.

ACCESS TO LOWER REGISTER Support the sound through a feeling of width in the back, getting wider as you descend. With one hand, feel the vibrations in the chest, which increase as you descend. Carry on down in semitones until surrender (sopranos and tenors can play until they drop out)! Use sounds like *yah*, *mah*, or any vowel.

TROMBONE TUNE Have fun with the lips and tongue by sliding up each rising pair of notes. Repeat in different keys.

MISSING LINK Sing numbers to a scale. When the signal is given, the note should be sung silently. For example: *one two [silence] four five six [silence] eight*. Keep changing and miss out more and more notes.

RELAX

Flex and relax your joints slowly, then repeat quickly. Concentrate in turn on your wrists, elbows, knees, shoulders, feet and ankles.

CHANGE YOUR SHORT PANTS

To revise onset (see **Tips and terms**, page 40), have fun with short pants. Laugh; *ha ha ha*, and repeat to a sequence of vowels, then pant silently.

VOWEL VARIATION WITH LIQUID LIPS

Change the vowel by rounding the lips. Sing *ah* and round the lips forward (becomes *o* as in *dog*, then *aw*, then *oo*). Sing to a scale up and down. Change the vowel on each note and then try the same exercise, to a chromatic scale.

STEPPING DOWN

Repeat this warm-up a semitone higher each time. Make sure the onset is clean and the vowels stay even as you descend.

WELLINGTON SONG

Flap the lips, then the tongue. Then sing the following in various keys:

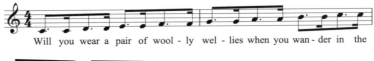

Will you wear a pair of wool-ly wel-lies when you wan-der in the

val-leys and the fol-ly of the wool-ly wel-ly wear-ing will be yours.

PASS THE PARCEL

In a choral context, all hum an agreed note. Then, starting at one end of the choir, each singer joins in one by one, receiving the sound from one neighbour and passing it to the neighbour on the other side. Try:

• Each person sings only when 'holding' the sound.

• Each person holds the note on until the end.

• The conductor directs when the sound is passed on, or back again.

SEEKING THE CALM CENTRE

Sit down silently, using only the leg muscles (not the back). Without speaking, each singer looks at and memorizes a short, chosen section of music. After thirty seconds, sing it from memory. Repeat to check for errors.

— SESSION 26 —

ELIMINATE THE SHOULDER TENSION

Raise one or both shoulders to the neck. Hold for different lengths of time and release slowly or quickly. Squeeze your face tight when your shoulders are up and relax it when they are down.

ROUND UP

Try this warm-up in canon at one bar/measure:

ni-nga-na   na-nga-na   no-nga-na   nu-nga-na   ne-nga   na-nga   ning   nong

Spin a lassoo over and round your head on each half-bar/measure.

KALEIDOSCOPE

Make up games, changing *ah* to *aw* to *oo* using your jaw and lips as well as tongue. Here are a few ideas:

- Change the vowel while slowly sliding up and down a fifth, then an octave.

- Repeat sliding up and down an octave firstly with everyone together, then with everyone at different speeds.

- Hold the notes of a major triad (individuals choose which). Slowly vary the vowels: *w-oo-aw-o-ah-è-i*.

HIT THE HIGH NOTES

Sing the vowel *ee* up a scale of G for five or six notes, and back. Repeat with the vowel *i* (as in *pig*). Start to darken the sound (towards *ear*) on E (see **Dark chocolate**, page 24).

Sing a whole octave scale of G, sopranos darkening on top E, F sharp, and G (the rest of the choir can sustain a chord of G to *ee*, then *i*). Try with tenors also darkening, and then without, to see which sound you prefer.

RURAL HARMONY

This warm-up needs sensuous consonants (see **Tips and terms**, page 40) with full support. Try it in canon at four bars/measures, and then repeat in E major, F major, G major, *etc.*

Down   in   a   val - ley,   cat - tle   are   gra - zing.

There   I   sit   and   dream____   of   you,   while

in - sects   are   buzz - ing   a - mong   the   boughs.

FACE SCREAM Make extreme faces: first scream silently, then squeeze your eyes and lips tightly shut, and change back again. Move your lips quickly from your brightest *ah* to their most forward *w* position (silently). Then massage the face and neck.

SNIGGERING SNAKE Hiss repeatedly with very short sounds (each lasting about half a second), with equal gaps between them. Do this all in one breath, continuing until the breath supply runs out. Check the lower abdomen, the chest and the sides of the waist for gentle movement as you hiss out. 'Think' the sound into the facial bones. Smile inside, but don't open your lips wide.

PLEASE RELEASE ME Make sure that the attack is clean, and release after each pair of notes. Choose your own vowel to sing to. Repeat a semitone higher each time to work the breathing mechanism naturally.

SLOW-MOTION HORSE RIDING Repeat the following warm-up four times, as follows: hum, *oo*, *aw*, *ya* (the vowel should start on the beat and renew on every beat). On the *ya* version, gently pull and release on each note. Repeat with staccato crotchets/quarter notes and legato minims/half notes, then vice versa.

 Hold the reins of a horse and pull on them gently as you sing.

LION'S ROLL Roll *rrrr* up and down as a siren. If this is a problem, use a lip trill (*brr*) or a *d d d* sound (repeated very quickly) instead. Repeat a favourite warm-up using *rrr* sounds before each vowel.

PARAGLIDER In pairs, or with the choir divided into two, hum in unison. One glides up to any high note, then rejoins the other who has held the original pitch. Change round.

CALM CENTRE Breathe in gently and slowly. Start with your arms at the sides, palms forward, slightly away from the body. As you breathe in, slowly raise your hands, bending them at the elbow. Imagine that you are wearing a flowing robe with heavy sleeves as you slowly raise your hands. Then imagine that you are holding a cup, a globe, or a sphere of light, and hold your breath and the object for a few seconds. Breathe out and gently release the object as you lower your hands again.

— SESSION 28 —

SWINGING THE TRUNK — Keeping the feet still, rotate your trunk slowly as if you are an elephant, looking behind you to the left and right. Let the muscles of the body move evenly and not too fast, thereby freeing the muscles that help support the sound.

ANGRY CAT — Hiss strongly for just a few seconds at a time. Hold your breath, release, and hiss again.

WATER SPORT — Sing the following as evenly as you can. Repeat to each vowel in turn, then with consonants, such as *la, ma, va, wa, ya, pa, ka, sma, dra, kra*. Then move up a semitone.

 Whilst singing, imagine you are on water-skis and gently pull on the rope, taking the weight in your whole body.

TRIPPING OFF THE TONGUE

Make up your own nonsense words for more verses—not in any way an Irish jig!

BLENDING GAME — Each chorister picks a random note and holds it, checking with each neighbour that there is a good clash of pitches. On a signal, all singers begin to slide the note until the pitches begin to match. Eventually, one note will naturally become the keynote. See if you can form a chord!

ELEVATION SENSATION — Imagine you are immersed in a tank of water and want to swim up using only your hands. Breathe in naturally. As you breathe out, put your palms together in front of you (as if praying) and glide upwards through the water. When fully stretched, turn your palms outwards and breathe in, lifting yourself with a strong swimming stroke outwards and down.

BACKWARD STRETCH   Standing tall, stretch backwards, touching your elbows together behind your back, and really stretch the shoulders.

 GOLDFISH BOWL   Waggle the jaw loosely like a fish, saying *yah yah yah*. Feel the hinge of the jaw move freely (test that the jaw rotates rather than moving forward by feeling with one finger on each side). Swim the sound up and down.

     Slowly imitate the movements of a fish.

 INTERVAL TASKS

① Sing each bar/measure to a vowel (change each bar/measure).
② Interval game: sing and name each pair.
③ Sing in canon.
④ Hold different notes in some voices while others go on. Make juicy blends.

 ITALIAN TEARS   Make sure that the consonants are clear and the phrase legato. Each vowel should be sung on the beat.

     Sob a little as you sing.

 THE LOST CHORD   In a choral context, make up a chord by using a number game, or letter names. For example: sing up a scale to five. Then find pitches one, three and five. Each person then chooses a number to sing—enjoy the blend. Swap notes with a neighbour, and enjoy the new blend. This way, the choir can begin to find their own note once the keynote has been given.

 TOTAL IMMERSION   Breathe in very slowly: imagine the breathing starts at the top of your head and slowly fills your body down to the ends of your toes. Then breathe out, feeling the air level rise again, with the last centimetre left at the top of your head.

— SESSION 30 —

RELAX

Try these relaxation games any time during warm-ups and rehearsals after a period of concentrated work.

- Jog gently, keeping your toes on the ground.
- Dance like a rag doll.
- Waggle your jaw, just lightly touching the hairs at the jaw hinge.

INNER TUBE

Try moving your stomach muscles without breathing. This sensation reinforces our awareness when we breathe. Now just breathe naturally and deeply and check the movement again.

LIFT GOING UP

Sing this warm-up to each vowel in turn:

FEEL GOOD

The following illustrates different types of vowel and consonant singing—pay particular attention to the articulation. Choristers can sing it in canon at two bars/measures (stop when all reach the pause).

Feel good! Feel fine! Stay now! Be mine! You know I care, no

doubt, I swear. You are my star._____

Take an imaginary shaker or rattle in each hand. Shake alternately or in patterns of your choice. Now punch in the air on each accent with alternate hands.

RETURN TO BASS

In a choral context, hum an agreed chord, then the whole choir slides up in pitch to the highest note that each individual can reach. Then slowly slide down again to find the original note.

TOTAL IMMERSION TWO

Repeat **Total immersion** (page 32) this time imagining that the air is a colour that is slowly filling you up.

CHICKEN STRUT   Whisper *woh who woh*, then *bwoh bwoh* flapping your lips and jaw ever more loosely. Flap your arms and shoulders too, and release all the muscles involved!

    Strut like a chicken.

HUMMED CONSONANTS   Revise the hummed consonants *mm*, *nn* and *ng*. Then sing the following three warm-ups separately; choristers can try all three together and in canon. Repeat using different vowels.

ma - nga ni - ba ni - ba   ma   ma - mbo

la la la la   la - nga

lam - bam ba____   ma - na - ma - na

SLUR AND LIFT   Sing this warm-up to each vowel in turn. Then start with a consonant, and go on to end with one too, for example: *ah bah bat*, following the slurs. Don't forget to lift at the very end too.

BLEND WITH YOUR NEIGHBOUR   Face a partner. Sing *ee* at an agreed pitch straight at each other and listen to how the sounds begin to merge.

INNER HARMONY   Sitting comfortably (or lying on your back), breathe slowly and then begin to hum a deep note. In a choral context, everyone else then slowly joins in with the same note or a concordant interval. Try it with your eyes shut, and concentrate on listening.

— SESSION 32 —

THE LEANING TOWER   In a standing position, let one arm fall to your side, pointing your fingers downwards while breathing out. Slowly lift the other arm over your head, pointing at the opposite shoulder. Lean sideways from your hips in the direction of this finger. Stretch to the comfortable limit, then repeat on the other side.

PAINT GUN POWER   Make your forefinger into a paint gun and extend your arm to paint a wall. Each time you press forward with your finger, hiss. Draw a large square in front of you, then a circle, then patterns of your choice. Now paint a picture, with short hisses/presses for dots as needed.

THIN ICE   Try the second note of each pair full length, then staccato—glide and release. Experiment with making up your own words, for example: *piya* or *mmba*. Choristers can try this as a canon in two parts.

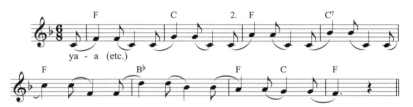

ya - a (etc.)

 Skate on the spot as you sing, one glide each half-bar/measure.

MONKEY PUZZLE   Make short sounds, like a monkey. Try the following with several vowels in turn, then change the vowel every two bars/measures, one bar/measure, half-bar/measure. Each note should have the same quality of tone as in legato singing.

sim.

GOLD BLEND   Repeat **Blend with your neighbour** (page 34). This time use *oo, ah, eh,* etc. Notice that the longer you do it, the closer the blend of sound (until you run out of breath!).

PARALLEL BARS   Choristers, make parallel motion chords by each choosing a note from a tonic triad. Then all slide up one degree of the scale together.

HARMONIC HEAVEN   Sitting comfortably (or lying on your back), sing vowels softly, gradually changing from one to another. Listen for the harmonics (see **Tips and terms**, page 40).

INCREDIBLE HULK

Raise your arms above your head, feeling how the ribcage lifts a little. Now slowly lower your arms to your sides, keeping the chest lifted. Your chest should stay in this position, even when breathing out.

ARM'S LENGTH

Hiss, whilst pushing against a wall. Use steady, firm arm weight in front of you. Repeat with *sh* and *ff*.

VOLUME CONTROL

Try this several times; first with a hum, then with *oo, aw, ah, eh* and *ee*. Repeat a semitone higher each time.

NOT DVOŘÁK

Sing the following to *ah*, then other vowels. Articulate clearly, concentrating on lifting and phrasing. Repeat in A minor, B minor, *etc*. Then repeat six times, breathing in between repetitions. Remember to breathe naturally, not gasp for breath—join the music up silently.

FEELING A LITTLE HORSE

Each chorister chooses to sing any note from a given triad. Slide the chord up, by ascending together in semitones. The sound should be lifted from the back, rather than the chin!

Press gently down onto a vaulting horse.

CHROMATIC SCALE

Sing to any vowel, then to *nn*. Check the tuning on the first note of every bar. Choristers can try repeating the warm-up in two-part canon, two bars/measures apart—then check the tuning on each note! Slur in pairs, first 1–2, 2–4, then 1, 2–3, 4–1, *etc*.

HOT HANDS

Hum a long note, holding the palms of your hands an inch or a couple of centimetres apart.

Feel the temperature between them. Gradually move them apart, keeping the feeling of connection between them.

ONLY YEW — Chew gently, whispering *yew yew yew* with extreme movement of cheeks and jaw, screwing up your eyes. Then release the jaw and facial muscles.

TOOTHPASTE TUBE — Breathe in and out, gently keeping the ribcage buoyant (imagine you are keeping the top of the toothpaste tube full while squeezing the bottom part). Feel the space between the bottom of the ribcage and the hips—give the support muscles (see **Tips and terms**, page 40) the room they need.

KEEPING AFLOAT — Try this whole piece to these sounds in turn: *ha, maw, i* (pig), *ww, blah, sfree*. Then choose your own sounds. Keep the ribcage actively buoyant throughout, ready for each new phrase.

VIBRATO GAME — (See **Tips and terms**, page 40). Sing alternating notes a semitone apart, to any vowel, or two alternate vowels, for example *eh* or *a-i-a-i*. Gradually increase the speed—see how fast you can get!

MIRROR IMAGE — Face a partner. Together, gradually sing through each vowel, slowly and carefully listening to the other person (*oo-aw-ah-eh-ee*). Not only will the vowel harmonics start to work together, but the pitch will match too.

FEELING DOMINANT — In a choral context, create the harmonic progression I–V–I, by moving one step or staying on one pitch (if the note is common to both chords). For example: in the progression C–G–C (I–V–I), sopranos stay on G, altos sing E–D–E, and tenors C–B–C. Basses can begin to master the hurdle of fourths and fifths by singing C–G–C. Then swap the parts around.

HOT DUO — Repeat **Hot hands** (page 36) with a neighbour. When the connection is there, start to move apart, and see how far you can step away and still feel it.

GROCERY BAGS Hold two heavy bags, keeping your shoulders back and straight. Breathe gently and keep the shoulders down.

 MOUTH AND JAW GAMES If your lips or jaw become tense, try the following:

- Extract a piece of meat from between your teeth.
- Be a fish.
- Smile and frown alternately.
- Dislodge a fly sitting on your chin, using only your facial muscles.

However, avoid extreme facial expressions when singing!

 HORSE SENSE Snort as if you are a horse—like *brr*, but more flappy! Go from a high sound to a lower one, repeating at a higher pitch each time.

 WIDTH OF THE VIB Sing a low note to *aw* with no vibrato. Start a slight tremolo, gradually increasing the width of the vibrato, then gradually narrowing it again. End with no vibrato as you started.

 LEGATO STROLL THROUGH THE RANGES Choose your own vowel. Aim for even tone throughout, as this will help with changes of register. (Solo singers can sing each part in turn.)

 COWBOY SONG Pay careful attention to the intonation. Try with some singers holding the first note of each bar/measure for the whole of that bar/measure, as an alternative.

dum - ba - di - nga (etc.)

 THE LOST CHORD Repeat **Feeling dominant** (page 37). Add another chord, such as IV or VI. Then add simple decorations. One good turn in the soprano part deserves another in the altos!

 MAGNETIC FIELD Hum a low note and move your hands around your head like a cap, then up and down your body like a cloak (about two centimetres from the body). Tap into your magnetic field!

— SESSION 36 —

 HANDBAGGING Swing your arms lightly, as if they have no power—only their weight. Then repeat with an imaginary handbag in each hand.

 VIBRATO GAME ① Sing alternate notes, as close to each other in pitch as you can (less than a semitone).
② Sing a single mordent, then hold the note on without vibrato.
③ Now sing a double mordent.
④ Now sing a short trill, followed by a long note without vibrato.
⑤ Now sing a long trill.

 MESSA DI VOCE Revisit **Volume control** (page 36), altering the colour as well as the volume. Now sing the following, first with a hum, then with *oo*, *aw*, *ah*, *eh* and *ee*.

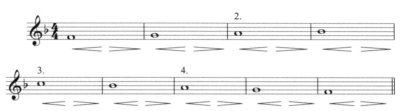

 Be a string player. Get louder by:

* Increasing the bow weight (support).
* Increasing the bow speed (lift of the sound).
* Increasing the vibrato.

 FORCE FOOD Sing this exercise through slowly to tune each interval. Choristers can then try it in a two-part canon, with the first part finally pausing on the last note until part 2 catches up.

Feed sa - la - mi to the ar - my give the na - vy wa - vy noo - dles

soaked in gra - vy.

 CHORD PROGRESS Add more chords to your harmonic progression, for example: I–IV–V–VI–II. The conductor can control the progression through shorthand signals. Add suspensions by delaying the movement of one of the parts.

 REACTIVATE Now do something very energetic to reactivate the adrenalin! Jog on the spot, or enjoy some animal calls.

Tips and terms

CONSONANTS   In speech and singing, consonants help to propel the airflow and therefore are of use both rhythmically and technically. Some are 'unvoiced', such as *p*, *t*, *k* and *s*. 'Voiced' consonants (where the larynx makes a sound) are much more important in singing than we may think. They have their own resonance, which:

- Improves the quality of the vowel sounds that follow.
- Makes words clearer (no more shouting at choirs for unclear words!).
- Provides internal rhythm to propel the music along.
- Creates a real legato through the minefield of words we have to negotiate.

DIPHTHONGS   As we shift from vowel to vowel, we encounter the natural diphthongs (two vowel sounds, for example: *late*, *eh-ee*), triphthongs (three vowel sounds, for example: *voyage*, *o-ee-eh*) and others from the thong family, which make up normal speech in English. For smooth singing we must decide which sounds need to be lengthened and which shortened.

HARD PALATE   This is the roof of the mouth (where the sound *ah* resonates particularly strongly).

HARMONICS   These are simply overtones of a basic note, which produce the tone qualities of any instrument or voice.

LARYNX   As well as an aid to breathing, eating and working, the larynx or 'voice box' is our musical instrument. It therefore needs to be treated gently (see **Support**, below). Its complex action needs more detail than can be covered here.

ONSET   The start of a sung sound is normally called the 'onset'. Some people call it 'attack' which is fine in the original Italian, but feels a little warlike for everyday use in English. It can be glottal (like a gentle cough), breathy (*haa*), or a combination of both. All three have their uses.

PHARYNX   The resonating chambers above the larynx (called the 'pharynx') are activated by the air/sound leaving the larynx. We can feel this resonance by touching the neck. (For example: *ee* feels especially tingly at the back, hummed sounds at the front.) The tongue, jaw and lips affect the sound after it leaves the pharynx.

SUPPORT   We use the word 'support' to cover everything underpinning the breathing mechanism, which enables us to sing with the whole apparatus. It means maintaining stability in the essentially non-moving parts of the body (back, head/neck, ribcage, legs, *etc.*) and facilitating the movement necessary for breathing (using the lower abdomen).

SOFT PALATE   To locate the soft palate, first close your lips and sing *mm*. Then open your lips and raise the front of the tongue to form *nn*, and then the back of tongue too, to make *ng*. Where the back of your tongue meets the roof of your mouth is the soft palate. If the soft palate is not raised effectively, the sound will be nasal and will alter in quality if you pinch your nose.

VIBRATO   Vibrato is a slight fluctuation in pitch and intensity (and a basic factor in our singing), helping to give voices their quality and individuality. It occurs naturally and should not be introduced artificially. Effective use of vibrato can enhance many musical styles. However, if it is very slow it makes a wobble, if too fast a tremolo, and if too wide, it sounds like a trill. In rehearsal, visit extremes to increase awareness.

VOWELS   Vowels are the main carriers of sound, forming the musical line and its tone quality. Linguists describe vowels in terms of 'front', 'central' and 'back' (or similar words) so think about which part of the tongue is lifted. Similarly, the words 'open' and 'closed' can describe the tongue position—down for open (*i* as in *this*) and up in the middle for closed (*ee*). A 'covered' vowel is where the high harmonics are excluded by rounding the lips or by simply releasing the jaw so that the extreme vowels (*ee* and *oo*) become more *aa* like. 'Modifying' a vowel means altering its tone quality to even its tone through the vocal ranges. It is often used to darken the sound of high soprano notes (to avoid screeching!).